Secrets of Becoming a Virtuous Woman

PROVERBS 31

By Dr. Kathy Lynn Yorkshire

Danielle,

As you continue your journey of becoming a virtuous woman, always remember there's nothing too hard for God, We may be limited but He is Limitless!

Sincerely,

Kathy Yorkshire

Secrets of Becoming a Virtuous Woman

Published by: Dr. Kathy Lynn Yorkshire

www.virtuouswomentoday.com

International Standard Book Number: 978-1-7369333-0-5

Cover Design: Jennyfer Villalta

Interior Design: Capitol Communications, LLC

Contents

Dedication

This book is dedicated to every woman who is resolved to be virtuous, God's way.

ↄ৪০

Luke 1:45 (NKJV)

45Blessed *is* she who believed, for there will be a fulfillment of those things which were told her from the Lord.

ↄ৪০

Esther 4:14 (AMP)

14For if you remain silent at this time, liberation and rescue will arise for the Jews from another place, and you and your father's house will perish [since you did not help when you had the chance]. And who knows whether you have attained royalty for such a time as this [and for this very purpose]?

Acknowledgements

Lord Jesus, it started with you giving me the vision and assignment to write this book. Throughout the journey of writing, you were there to encourage and empower me when I felt inadequate and discouraged. You strengthened me (spiritually and physically) in my weak moments. At every turn you were there to remind me when I "forgot" that while I am limited in my natural abilities, you are limitless. Thank you for every challenge along this journey. You revealed yourself every time and I give you glory for all of it!

To the host of family and friends who encouraged, challenged and prayed me through the completion of this project, I am so very grateful for you. My Beta-readers: Candice, Deloris, Frances, Ted and Wanda. Your individual and constructive feedback was priceless in the book's development. It helped me to see so much better from the reader's perspective and I am very thankful for you and your support. To Chris from Blue Square Writers, your input was priceless and it set me on a clear path. To Karlyn from Capitol Communications, I could not have asked for a better designer for the layout of the interior of my book. From our first conversation, you were not only attentive to every detail but you were very patient with me through every phase. I learned so much from you and I am extremely pleased with the outcome. To my cover designer, Jennyfer, wow, just wow! The way God gave you the vision for the cover design still amazes me. I recall telling you what the book was about and I asked you to pray. Our God delivered beyond what we could have imagined. Thank you for listening and helping to bring forth the vision.

Secrets of Becoming a Virtuous Woman

PROVERBS 31

Preface

The Secret of Our YES

T
he virtuous woman is resolute in her decision to say **yes** to God and
she is in continual pursuit for His will for her life. I recall a time
when I desperately desired a stronger relationship with Him. I was
tired of the "same ole same ole" life as usual. In addition to fasting, intentional
prayer and study time, I read a book entitled, *Secrets of the Secret Place* by Bob
Sorge. In all of this, God's response was to seek Him above all else and that
period in my life was the start of major transformation. He connected me with
someone who I had no idea would become a dear friend and prayer sister.
Her name is Clementine and she came alongside me to read and study *Secrets
of the Secret Place*. We met weekly to pray and discuss it, chapter by chapter.
More about my sister, Clementine, later.

During this pivotal season of seeking the Lord, He gave me peace in
restlessness. I prayed and asked God to renew my mind. The Bible says,
"And do not be conformed to this world, but be transformed by the renewing of your mind that you may prove what *is* that good and acceptable and
perfect will of God."[1] It also says, "Seek first the Kingdom of God and all
His righteousness, and all these things will be added."[2] A number of years
ago, I was looking for another position. I had two interviews several months
apart. I was so confident during the interview for one of the positions (where
I was employed) and I had the support of my supervisor as well as the hiring
manager. A few months after the interview, I was told one of our top-level
executive did not think I was qualified, although, the search committee and
other colleagues voted for me. Needless to say, while I was very disappointed
initially, I became aware that it wasn't my time to change positions. You see, I
prayed before applying for the new role and I asked God to close the door if
it was not His will. That remained my prayer throughout the entire process.

Over the course of the following year, some of the people who voted for me to get the position came to my office to express their disappointment for how things turned out. As a child of God, I retorted, "God said He will close a door that no one can open and He will open a door no one can close"[3] and that promise gave me so much peace. Although, I had peace, in my mind, I still thought there was something else for me to do besides what I was doing. I wanted a change. So a few months later, I resumed my job search. My friend and prayer partner, Clementine, visited my office one day and I told her about my thoughts and actions. She said, "Doctor Kathy, you are too anxious. Do not apply for any more positions and seek God for direction." I knew she was right and I yielded to her wisdom. That moment changed the course of the next season in my life. You see, in retrospect there was a void in my life and I thought another position would fill it. But, God had other plans and they included me being focused on Him and His will (also known as His purpose for my life). This was certainly a pivotal moment in my life and in my walk with Him. God wanted me to place Him first above everything else including searching for a new position. Later, I realized that it was nothing more than a distraction because where He had me was where He assigned me and my assignment was not over just because I was ready to move on. Seeking Him and making Him first in my life was the essential element and action I needed to experience a renewed mind and transformation.

Right now, is there something you know God wants you to do but you're too focused on what you want? If so, please stop and reconsider. Say **"yes"** to God and His will for your life. He promises to not let you down. We may not understand why He closes certain doors in our lives but we can be certain of His protection because He knows what's on the other side. He always has our best interest in mind and He doesn't want us to abandon our assignments prematurely. Why? Because those assignments are connected to our purpose.

Jesus Christ has invited us to a living and evolving relationship with Him. Have you said yes to His invitation? If so, what did you do to begin cultivating the relationship? In other words, beyond saying yes, what have you done to get to know Christ in an intimate way? Building quality relationships whether personally or professionally require effort, trust and time. Think about those personal and professional relationships you have built previously or those you are building now. What happened after you responded with your "yes" (in word or action)? Where did the relationships lead? Did one of your high school teachers or college professors eventually become a mentor to you? Did you find that good girlfriend or buddy that you could trust no matter what? Did an associate casually turn out to be one of your most powerful prayer and accountability partners?

Over time, our relationship with some people strengthens. That is exactly what God wants us to experience with Him. First, we must say yes and then we must take action. Faith without works (the action) is ineffective.[4] Sister, it is dead. Sometimes standing still is the action (the works) and God will give you the discernment to know. More about that later. The virtuous woman accepts her challenges and she does not quit. We must prioritize our relationship with God and everything else in our lives will flow. Think about at least one thing that has challenged you in cultivating a better relationship with God? For me it was time. I was busy and had not adjusted everything on my "plate" to make the time.

Speaking of time, my life situation reminded me of the sisters Mary and Martha. The word of God explains the story in Luke 10:39–42 (AMP):

> [39]She had a sister named Mary, who seated herself at the Lord's feet and was *continually* listening to His teaching. [40]But Martha was very busy *and* distracted with all of her serving responsibilities; and she approached Him and said, "Lord, is it of no concern to you that my sister has left me to do the serving alone? Tell her to help me *and* do her part." [41]But the Lord replied to her, "Martha, Martha, you are worried and bothered *and* anxious about so many things; [42]but *only* one thing is necessary, for Mary has chosen the good part [that which is to her advantage], which will not be taken away from her."

Admittedly, when I made the decision to say yes, things began to change in a noticeable way. Especially when I spent time with God. I began to put things after God that I would normally have put before Him. I wanted a more authentic yes to God so that I could draw closer to Him and Him to me. You might think you have too much to do to make time to pray and study God's word but from what I've learned, we cannot afford NOT to make the time. Why? We are limited, but He is limitless.

Of course, I still face challenges and recognize when my focus is out of order. Mary and Martha's story helps me identify distractions. Later, I will elaborate and share more of my personal experiences. I pray they will help you seek God like never before as you are either ending a season in your life or as you find yourself entering a new season. Who knows, you just might be reading this while in the middle of a particular season. God does not make mistakes and His timing is impeccable. It is no surprise to Him that you are reading this book at this time of your life and I believe it is a part of His plan.

This is my prayer for you:

Heavenly Father, the One who created us. The one who knew us before we were formed in our mothers' wombs I come before your throne of grace on behalf of each and every one of my sisters reading this book. God you knew they would hold it at this very moment. You knew who would need encouragement and who would need to read about some of my personal struggles and testimonies because of what they have experienced or may be experiencing right now. You are a good, good father and I praise your holy and matchless name. May each and every word in this book bless my sisters in a mighty way. More than I could ever have imagined. I thank you for speaking to each one of us with your word as we pray, fast, and as we seek your kingdom and all of its righteousness first before any of our own personal desires. My God, I am so excited about what you are going to do in the lives of my sisters. I pray that I will meet some of them one day if it is your will. I thank you Father because you loved us so much and you will do whatever it takes to get our attention. I thank you and I honor you. May you continue to get the glory by the fruit of our lips and by the work of our hands in Jesus' mighty name, I seal this prayer on behalf of my sisters. Amen, amen and amen.

Introduction

In this book, I encourage you to go after God like never before as you
desire to identify and fulfill your purpose. It will aid you in being resolute to seek God, His Kingdom and all His righteousness first, just as
He commanded all of His children to do.[5] Throughout this book, I refer to
my Savior, Jesus Christ, as God, Christ, Lord and Jesus. If you have received
the gift of salvation and if you believe and apply the principles that I share
with you from the Bible, by faith, your life will change. You will embark on a
shift, a beautiful transformation in your walk with God as you live out your
purpose. As we explore the life of the virtuous woman this book will be used
as a resource for you to do so in a practical way.

The virtuous woman described in this book fears the Lord with a reverential fear and she has made the decision to abide in Him. She can do all
things through Christ who strengthens her. That is the very definition of a
virtuous woman: woman of strength. You might not feel very strong right
now but rest assured that you are not alone. While writing this book, there
have been times when I have not felt strong at all: physically, mentally or
spiritually. Nevertheless, God's word and His grace prevailed, evidenced by
this book that is based on my biblical study, personal relationship and amazing
experiences with Him. Furthermore, I share many of my moments of reflection
and I invite you to do the same. At the end of each chapter there is a section
entitled, *For Consideration and Action* so you can reflect on your own life and
take appropriate action.

The life of a virtuous woman is not a checklist for perfection. Rather,
becoming a virtuous woman is a life-time of work in progress. She understands
her position in managing her home (single or married) and serving in her
community and ministry. She cultivates her relationship with God and focuses
on being in lock step with Him. Therefore, the application of scripture in her
life is priority. Does she get it wrong at times? Absolutely! Thank God for
His grace, forgiveness and chances to start anew. Especially, when she comes
to Him with a repenting heart and a teachable spirit.

According to the Old Testament Hebrew Lexicon, Proverbs 31:10–31 is an acrostic poem where each line begins with a letter of the Hebrew alphabet in order. In verses 10–31, King Lemuel recites wise counsel (given by his mother) about the type of woman he should desire to marry: a noble, virtuous woman and disciple of Jesus Christ. It's important to note that she is not just one woman. She is many women. Women of the biblical era and women today who have one most important thing in common—their love of Christ. While the virtuous woman's faults and life's challenges are not necessarily highlighted in Proverbs 31, we know she encountered them. Virtuous women today encounter them. The key (and her secret) is she knows the source of her redemption, peace, and strength. That is Jesus Christ, her Lord and Savior. He empowers her with wisdom and grace to accomplish so much especially to bless those around her and in doing so, He gets the glory.

In this book, I break down verses 10 through 31 in an understandable and achievable way that will allow you to make practical application in your life. As you read and respond to the reflection prompts at the end of each chapter, please remember nothing surprises God. He wants us to focus on Him and not the things that surprise us. For instance, distractions, our shortcomings and seemingly impossible situations. The virtuous woman is hopeful and optimistic because of her trust in Christ and confidence in His word. Simply stated, based on the acrostic poem, this book describes how God transforms the modern-day woman who desires to be virtuous, His way. Transformation occurs as a result of her decision to first say yes to God and to honor Him by how she honors her friends, family, and the people in her community. She understands that He blesses her so she may bless others whether she is married or not, with or without children. She has learned to be content in each God-appointed season she experiences. Are you ready to begin your transformational journey? Begin by turning to the next page.

Chapter 1

Proverbs 31:10

**A wife of noble character who can find?
She is worth far more than rubies.**

The virtuous woman is an admirable, exceptional, and mighty woman. God treasures her and adores her more than cherished jewels. Precious gems do not come close to her value because she offers so much to so many. She brings her desires and goals before God and seeks His guidance because she knows what He has and wants for her is better than she could ever imagine. She understands that He has connected her to certain people for a reason and they have a role to play in her destiny and vice versa.

I wanted to write a book for a very long time but never imagined this one. But God knew. In 2019, during a discipleship session with one of my prayer sisters, Frances, I gave her an update on writing this book and I explained that my next book would be a devotional. That same night, I was speaking with a publisher about my progress and struggles. I told her that the book was not as streamlined as I had planned. She read the draft and echoed my comments. She asked me a series of questions but one in particular stood out: "What do you think the problem is with what you wrote thus far and what are you feeling about the process?" I explained that in the process of writing my first book, I have identified at least one other book. A devotional. The publisher responded, "Some parts of your manuscript took me away from your main points to other parts of the Bible. That was hard to do because I found myself connected with what God said about the virtuous woman and your personal stories related to her." Next, she followed with this bomb, "Perhaps you have been writing two books all along. Your main book and a devotional." Oh my! She was spot on because that was not the devotional I initially envisioned! That was a revelatory moment that hit me so clearly. I recall during one of our prayer meetings a couple of years earlier, Clementine said, "I believe God is going to have you write many books and that you will write two simultaneously." I had no idea.

There were other times when I could see God moving in my life and I knew I had to trust the process knowing He would send destiny helpers. When I earned my master's degree people asked if I would ever pursue a doctorate. I always responded sternly, "No way!" I never desired a doctorate degree and I said that I would never get one. Ha! God must have been laughing at me because I spoke as if I was really in control of my life. After all, I accepted Him as my Lord and Savior, asking Him to order my steps and telling Him that I would submit to His will. I had worked in higher education for approximately ten years when out of nowhere, I felt depleted like I had nothing more to give to my students. I wondered if I should consider obtaining new skills, getting a certificate or attending professional development conferences. In any case, I longed to be a student again. I prayed about it a lot and did not realize I was embarking upon a never say never lesson. During that time, things began to happen that caught my attention; students and colleagues began to address me as Dr. Yorkshire in public and via email. This never happened before and unbeknownst to me, the confirmations would continue. One of my students addressed me as Dr. Yorkshire on the cover page of his assignment. I taped it to my wall in my home office for some years so I did not lose sight of what God was doing. Although I never had the desire to earn a doctorate, I believed in those moments, God was confirming His will for my life.

In 2010, I was selected to receive a faculty excellence award. My dean at the time stopped by my office and said "Congrats on your award. Now, all you need to do is get your doctorate." Wow, here we go again, I thought. So, I sought counsel from others, including several mentors and colleagues who earned their doctorates. I learned much from their individual feedback, insight and suggestions. One of my mentors recommended that I research one of the doctoral programs at Morgan State University. However, I did not think their programs would work for my schedule. Especially, with having two toddlers at that time. She mentioned it to me at least twice and I ignored it. One day while in the office, I received an all-staff email stating that the administrators of Morgan State would be visiting to share information about their Higher Education program curriculum. I attended the information session, applied for admission and the rest is history. God wants His desires for us to become our desires and He shares that in His word.[6] While we have free will to choose, He wants us to choose His way in His time. We should discern what that is by praying, studying His word and walking by faith.

This admirable woman intentionally seeks to develop herself in *every* area of her life. That includes advanced education and training for spiritual, professional and personal growth. She knows God has the master plan for all of it. In 2019, I participated in two small book study groups. In one group, we studied the lives of Esther and Ruth. We gleaned so much from the study and agreed to continue our study of other women of the Bible. The following week, I received an invitation from a local church ministry that my girlfriend attends, to learn more about their Queen Esther discipleship class. I knew immediately it was God telling me to move forward with the studies and He was showing me just how to do it. I attended the information session, completed the interest form and just like I mentioned earlier, the rest is history. The lesson for me remains the same. We are so precious to God, He wants His desires for us to become our desires, and while we have free will, He wants us to choose His way. Furthermore, we must discern what His way is, which is why prayer and study of scripture is key. I know I said this before but I strongly believe that it bears repeating.

For consideration and action:

Think about how verse ten below resonates with you personally. It doesn't matter if you are a wife or not. You are a woman first.

A wife of noble character who can find?
She is worth far more than rubies.

How else might you describe her as you reflect on the verse? Write them below.

she is...   *she is...*

_____   _____

Chapter 2

Proverbs 31:11–12

Her husband has full confidence in her and lacks nothing of value. She brings him good, not harm, all the days of her life.

The virtuous woman seeks God to learn ways that she can bring good to her husband. That good is described as her love, trustworthiness, integrity, prudence, her diligence, kindness and humility. Her husband obtains favor because she is a good wife.[7] Some years ago, Ted and I, along with several other married couples at my church completed an assessment on the five love languages. Since then, Ted and I have completed the assessment at least twice. This activity coupled with discussion has given me insight and understanding about what his love languages are and how I can respond to them on a day to day basis. For example, by expressing how much I love and appreciate his efforts around the house. Ted washes and folds clothes and I have often taken those things for granted. He needs to know and I tell him that it has not gone unnoticed. Therefore, I address one of his love language, words of affirmation.

The virtuous woman does not worship her husband's every move nor is she a "yes woman" who agrees with all of his decisions and perspectives. However, she does respect his right to have them. What doesn't sit right with her spirit, she takes it to the Lord in prayer. She shares wisdom and gives gentle guidance when needed, even at times when he doesn't want it. She calms and comforts him with kind words when he feels the weight of the world on his shoulders. She lifts him with words of encouragement during the times when he doesn't walk in confidence. What she speaks into his life builds him up and does not tear him down. Simply stated, she demonstrates her love for him unconditionally. Her husband understands that her role in his life brings enhancement. He recognizes that she sows strong seeds in her family and household. She affirms him, supports his goals and desires, speaks life into his circumstances, she prays with him and intercedes for him.

I often intercede for my husband during my personal prayer and worship time. I declare God's promises over his life. I let him know from time to time so he is aware that I cover him when I am in the secret place. I also pray for him when we touch and agree in prayer and as we bring his concerns before the Lord. This is important because he needs to experience my prayers to God on his behalf. Moreover, scripture says when two or three gather together in the name of Jesus, He promised to be in the midst of them.[8]

If you are not married, your position is special and unique. You are called to live in a committed relationship with the Lord (as your husband)[9] and in doing so, He wants you to identify and cultivate your spiritual gifts.[10] It is important that you understand your gifts. You may have the gift of teaching, leading, administration, prophesy, exhortation, and evangelism among others. Once you know what they are, ask God to show you how those gifts are connected to your purpose and especially, in this season of your life. If you have never completed a spiritual gifts (also called gifts of the spirit) assessment, please consider doing so.

Scripture says your gifts are manifested to be used for the common good.[11] But if you don't know what they are, how do you know they are being used (in your church, workplace, school and social organizations) and for the benefit or good of others through your ministry or service? The married woman should also be operating in her gifts but it is especially important to note that the unmarried woman's season of "singleness" gives opportunity and freedom to fully devote herself to God's call on her life without having the additional responsibilities of marriage. Married or unmarried, being able to bring good to someone else's life is empowering and powerful. Others should consider you as something good and a benefit to their lives.

For consideration and action: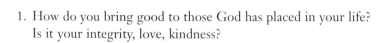

1. How do you bring good to those God has placed in your life? Is it your integrity, love, kindness?

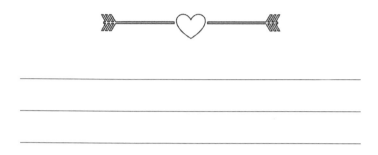

_____

_____

_____

2. If you are married, how do verses 11 and 12 resonate with you?

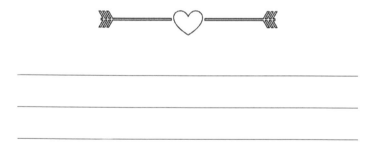

_____

_____

_____

3. In what **new** ways can you bring good to your husband? Jot down examples of how you will apply them in your life.

_____

_____

_____

4. If you are not married and you desire to be married, begin to pray and ask God if it is His will. Ask Him to help you further develop those attributes you noted for number one above well before He brings you a husband.

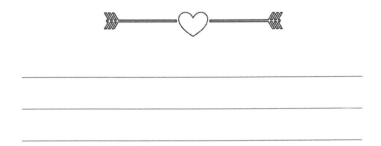

_____

_____

_____

Chapter 3

Proverbs 31:13

**She selects wool and flax
and works with eager hands.**

The virtuous woman doesn't mind helping when and where needed. Researching, pondering and preparing to help her family and community in ways God leads her. When I was single and living at home with my parents, I started a resume writing business. At the time, I was in a graduate program and working as a Human Resources assistant for a non-profit organization. God gave me a vision to start a business to help others with their resumes and cover letters. I immediately had clients; friends, family members and referrals. I also facilitated resume writing and interviewing workshops at women's shelters and public libraries. I earned additional income but I also volunteered my time doing what I enjoyed, helping others realize their goals.

The virtuous woman doesn't mind working with her hands in and outside of her home. I recall a time approximately twenty years ago when I served as the leader of the employment ministry at my church. We organized the church's first job fair. It was open to our congregation and members of the community. It was a success as some people made professional connections and were offered employment. The virtuous woman understands that her hands were created to execute the vision God gave her. The virtuous woman leads. She doesn't sit back and wait for opportunities, she inquires of God and creates them.

In 2013, while taking a walk on a beautiful day in August, my friend Tranishia and I felt strongly that the Lord called us to do something together with and for women. We did not have details but we prayed and waited. In 2014, at an event at Tranishia's home, God confirmed that we needed to move forward. Shortly after, Tranishia said she kept hearing the word **goal** in her spirit. While praying for a theme or name of the Expo, God gave me GOAL, which stands for Go On and Live. We took the plunge and scheduled our first official fellowship in March that same year. We had a nice time with several other ladies including another one of my dear friends Crystal, and we began to network and share ideas. As the Lord would have it, one of the ladies said, "We should plan an Expo." At that time, she had no idea of what the Lord had already revealed to Tranishia and me.

Go On and Live was birthed out of our prayers asking God to direct our paths and to help us use our spiritual gifts, purpose and business acumen for His glory and the edification of His people. After six months of planning we hosted the Expo in 2015 in a mid-size ballroom at a local hotel. The objective was to offer support to women entrepreneurs by providing an opportunity for them to promote and sell their products and services as well as to network with others.

Be mindful that life is going to keep happening while you are working on a God-given project. During this entire process my dad became very ill. I was on an emotional rollercoaster and physically exhausted while having to plan this event and essentially become his caregiver alongside my mom. He passed away a couple of weeks prior to our event and I honestly did not think I could still participate in the Expo. Some questions and thoughts ran through my mind:

1. What would Daddy want me to do? He would not want me to wallow in my devastation and sadness.

2. How can I let the other ladies down by not participating? Although they would totally understand if I didn't participate, I felt obligated to finish what WE started.

As I mentioned early on in this book, nothing surprises God. Absolutely nothing. He reminded me that what He started in me, He would finish. It was humbling to bless women who like me, want to Go On And Live. While we have not hosted another Expo since then, I am grateful for such a powerful experience and the grace God gave me to help carry out a vision He gave to us.

For consideration and action:

Are you eager and diligent with your work? You may not select wool and flax but what do you need in order to build and create something? Also, what opportunities have you prayed about or are you waiting for someone else to initiate them?

Perhaps God wants you to take the first step. Are you in prayer about it and do you keep feeling the push to align your actions with your faith? Have you received any confirmation? I feel like someone is reading this and saying, "Yes, I have received many confirmations." Then, I pray that you will discern the hand of God in your life with clarity and peace and make the decision to move forward.

Opportunities I am praying about now:

1. _____
_____
2. _____
_____
3. _____
_____

What I need or desire to get started (resources, people, etc.):

1. _____
_____
2. _____
_____
3. _____
_____

Confirmations I have received thus far, along with the date:

1. _____

_____

2. _____

_____

3. _____

_____

Chapter 4

Proverbs 31:14

**She is like the merchant ships,
bringing her food from afar.**

The virtuous woman shops on a mission and she looks to Jesus to be her shopping partner. She will travel the distance to obtain healthy food (organic, natural and plant-based). She may even plan to visit a farmer's market in order to get the freshest fruits and vegetables. To the extent possible, she will set aside additional money in her budget to pay the higher cost for her natural, organic and fresh food selections. Personally, I have done that for my family and as a result we have reduced the amount of times we eat out. This gives me more flexibility in my grocery shopping.

Bulk shopping at stores are cost saving options and I incorporate bulk shopping into my schedule on average, twice per month. My shopping habits and routine changed over time. It took years of trying different stores and shopping schedules to find what works best in this season of my life. Eating out often with two kids strained our finances and we found trying different things saves us money and presents healthier options over time. Now, eating out is more of a "special" occasion as opposed to what used to be the norm just a few years ago. That works for me and my household but you must consider what works for you.

If the virtuous woman is extremely busy and finds herself wrestling with having time to plan meals and cook them, she might try meal service kits as a way to save time. These kits provide step-by-step recipes and items needed to prepare meals and they are delivered to your door. For some women, this is a better option than actually researching recipes online or purchasing cookbooks and spending endless hours in the grocery store trying to figure it all out. Some of you may be couponing experts; I am not. Whatever the case, this focused woman identifies the best meal options for her household and budget. I have found that it helps me greatly to stay under or within budget. However, I have to resolve in my mind that I will not deviate from the shopping list. This is not always an easy plan but doable. If you are shopping for big ticket items, consider waiting for them to go on sale. Stores offer sales throughout the year and during the holiday season. God wants us to be profitable in our shopping and we should inquire of Him daily so that we move in wisdom. He is our advocate who promises to generously give us wisdom when we ask Him for it.[12] He also promises to order our steps.[13] So, keep your eyes and ears open.

For consideration and action: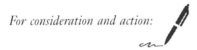

If not grocery shopping, what shopping challenges do you have? Do you indulge in too much "retail therapy" and need to scale back? God knows I have been there. When you go to the store do you find that you often leave with way too many items, many of which you "could not" resist? Consider creating a list to stay on track when planning your next visit. What adjustments can you make in your life that will afford you better results (financially, time and health-wise)? Below, write down two of your current struggles and actions you will take to overcome them. Remember, Jesus is your rock.

Struggle

_____

To overcome, I will _____.

Struggle

_____

To overcome, I will _____.

Chapter 5

Proverbs 31:15

**She gets up while it is still night;
she provides food for her family
and portions for her female servants.**

The virtuous woman rises early to speak to God and commit her day to Him. I am still working on the "rising early" part. She plans reasonably and manages her time effectively. As the keeper of her home, she understands her priorities and knows how to discern and minimize distractions. The virtuous woman organizes her life and when she is challenged in that area, she admits that she is overwhelmed and asks for help. Sister, we tend to consider it a badge of honor when we run around like a crazy person attempting to tackle every single thing, every single day. The laundry, dishes, making our beds, shopping for all the food and then preparing every meal. I used to feel so proud of myself when I operated with that mindset.

In the previous chapter we learned the importance of having flexibility in our shopping and that it is absolutely okay to change our routines in different seasons. The virtuous woman cared for her maids and she assigned tasks to them. In life today, I liken this to hiring a cleaning service to help with household organization, chores and as a way to reduce stress. Some years ago, after a long period of suffering from growing and annoying fibroids, I had a partial hysterectomy. My doctor informed me that I would be recovering for a minimum of six weeks. I knew that in order for me to fully relax, I wanted my house to undergo a major cleaning before I returned from the hospital. Sister, that was one of the BEST decisions I made. There is something that refreshes me about the smell of citrus disinfectant all throughout my house after the floors have been mopped, tubs and sinks scrubbed, and the counters and windows wiped. When the cluttered areas in my house are cleared, my mind is also cleared and I don't feel weighed down. I feel invigorated. Ted and I factored in the cost in our monthly budget so we could maintain a regular house cleaning schedule. You might implement other "stress free" hacks that work for you and your household. For instance, help with meal planning and delivery services, laundry service or lawn care. Also, you might take a day to rest alone. Schedule an appointment at the spa, spend a day reading a book or take a long walk. Do what energizes your mind, refreshes your spirit and gives you peace. Most times all I need is a conditioning clay mask or hot oil treatment in my hair while I paint my nails and toes. All of us have different needs and desires but the "take away" here is to do what works for you.

For consideration and action:

If you have not yet implemented anything, think about what gives you anxiety or makes you feel overwhelmed. Find at least one scripture that speaks to your situation and meditate on it daily. Write it down along with at least two ways you can overcome. I believe you will begin to see a shift before you know it.

Makes me feel anxious or overwhelmed:

_____

The scripture promise that I will declare over my life and apply:

_____

Two ways I can overcome:

_____

_____

Chapter 6

Proverbs 31:16

**She considers a field and buys it;
from her profits she plants a vineyard.**

The virtuous woman seeks Godly wisdom instead of just a good idea. She diligently stewards well the things God has put in her heart and in her hands. As an entrepreneur she delights in her God-given creativity and the harvest it yields. Therefore, she wisely invests her financial resources. I admit, there have been times when I missed the mark but, I am so grateful to God for the experiences and lessons learned along the way! I'm better because of them. From 2005 to 2009, my husband and I worked as realtors. We had two toddlers at that time and we welcomed the ability to earn additional income. As The Yorkshire Team, we worked for an awesome brokerage. During that time in the business, we closed numerous deals and we developed some professional relationships.

In 2006, Ted and I partnered with a group of other realtors to open another office within the same brokerage. We took out a home equity line of credit and partnered with a group of four others. We ultimately found two offices, signed two leases and began recruiting agents. But, little did we know, the market would soon tank and business would come to a screeching halt. We felt like we were "hemorrhaging" money to stay afloat and after a couple of months, our group could no longer afford to pay rent at both office locations so we tried to get out of the lease agreements. The broker of one of the leases allowed us to do so. Thank you, Jesus! But, the building owner of the other lease would not allow us to back out. Ultimately, we defaulted on that lease. For almost seven years Ted and I received "nasty grams" from the building owners and their attorneys regarding the first office lease. Finally, in 2013, the building owner sued us. Ted and I hired an attorney who attempted to help us settle for a far less amount of what we owed. She stressed that we offer an amount that we could realistically pay and if they did not accept it, she strongly encouraged us to file for bankruptcy. Filing for bankruptcy never crossed my mind and I did not want to do it. But when our attorney explained that if we didn't, the building owner's attorney would begin the process to garnish our paychecks, I immediately got out of my pity party. After all, we had children to take care of and a mortgage to pay. Our settlement offer was declined and we agreed to file for bankruptcy.

Ted and I prayed for so long to have this debt canceled. I thought perhaps the Lord sent the impending bankruptcy as a "raft" to keep us from drowning and I thanked Him for it. We scheduled to sign the papers on Monday. Well, the Thursday prior, our attorney sent me a text informing me that "there was a development in our case that she needed to apprise us of." I said a quick prayer, thanking the Lord for being in control because I thought she had something negative to report. When I called her back, she explained that the other partners and the building owner had reached a settlement. Our attorney also said, "as long as they pay the settlement by September, the building owner will release the judgment from you and Ted." I asked her to say that again. She repeated it and said, "they will release you and Ted from the debt as long as the others do not default and as long as you and the others DO NOT FILE BANKRUPTCY between now and September." I told her that I needed to put her on hold so I could have a praise break! She said she wanted to shout herself when the other attorney told her. To think we were about to accept the "raft" we thought would prevent us from drowning and our Savior had an even better way to protect and save us. There's no question that we make our own plans but it is the Lord who directs our steps.[14] Grateful, I am.

Ted and I experienced financial loss and a broken business partnership. Yet, we are thankful for God's mercy and grace. We did not file bankruptcy and we were forgiven a debt. Hallelujah! Glory to God! Our affiliation with the real estate company was an overall great experience and everything we encountered worked (and continues to work) for our good. Although we are no longer active agents, we receive profit share earnings almost every month. Profit share is a benefit offered to agents who remain at that brokerage for at least three years. That additional income has come in handy for things like unexpected veterinary bills, house repairs, and random date nights. While we experienced a business venture that did not work out, God promised to work everything—good and bad, for our good.[15] We stood on it. Our faith was strengthened even as we faced a "fall" with our business. There are a few key additional points that I want to bring to your attention:

1. We were scheduled to sign the bankruptcy papers just two or three days after receiving news that our debt would be forgiven. Talk about an on time God.

2. We signed a seven year lease. In the seventh year, the year the lease would end is when we were informed of the debt forgiveness. Ted and I looked for debt cancellation scriptures that we could stand on for this situation. Every time we received a "nasty gram" in the mail, I would thank God for His deliverance and write on it, UNLIMITED POSSIBILITIES FOR GOD.

3. Even in less than ideal circumstances, God still provides and makes ways.

Will we choose to focus on the less than ideal circumstances or will we acknowledge God's protection and provision in the middle of them? Our praise about God's goodness in our lives must be much louder than our temper tantrums and pity parties. When we fall, we must get up and take a step forward. I call it *active* faith. Think about how you demonstrate active faith in the midst of unwanted situations and circumstances. Do you allow yourself to stay "stuck" to the point where you do absolutely nothing? While doing all you know to do, are you calling out to God, declaring His word over your situations and waiting with great expectation for Him to do the seemingly impossible?

I hope my story encourages you in some way. God has a track record and He is always behind the scenes working on our behalf, charting our course and ordering our steps (even when we mistakenly step off). We must trust Him in all of it. Yes, all of it. That includes our failures, falls, mistakes and most vulnerable moments.

Experiencing God is not going to always look like a sunny day with blue skies and melodious sounds of birds singing. Side note, as I write this section, I hear birds singing to each other right outside my window and it's so tranquil to me. They seem to be so at peace, something I ask God to grant me on a daily basis. But, experiencing God when my circumstances and things around me are not peaceful can be so powerful. Why? You might ask. It's because that is when I really get to trust and rely on Him to move in those unpeaceful situations. What's more amazing is when I see the word of God active in my life. Remember, the virtuous woman declares His word over her life and she prays the scriptures over her family and household because her hope is in Him.

For consideration and action:

Identify and write down one thing you believe God is allowing you to do but based on other things happening in your life, you need to ask Him about timing. If you are unsure about this, identify and write down something you are praying about and you need to hear from God to assure it is His will (at this time or even at all).

_____

_____

_____

_____

_____

_____

_____

_____

Chapter 7

Proverbs 31:17

**She girds herself with strength,
and strengthens her arms.**

The virtuous woman understands the power of the secret place and she adamantly and consistently makes time to spend with God. It is God's desire that the virtuous woman is strengthened spiritually, mentally and physically because He wants her to prosper in those areas. It is important for the virtuous woman to begin her day in God's presence where she can speak to Him, hear from Him and worship Him. In doing so, she declares order and victory over her day knowing that it is His grace that will prevail.

While early morning suggests the most productive time, for some, it may be evening. The emphasis is that we must set aside time to be alone with God. The early morning time is a challenge for me because typically I like to sleep in. However, I recognize the importance of spending time with the Lord and I have been praying and asking Him to help me to become more consistent at seeking Him very early. Most mornings my time with the Lord consists of me on the couch where I talk to Him, meditate and reflect on Him. Sometimes it is with a song that ministers to me and other times I use the moments to be still and quiet. I often find myself rejoicing and thanking God. I call it my devotional time where I sing, cry and offer praise to Jesus. On occasion while listening to "Waymaker" by Michael Smith, I reflect on ways God has made and times He provided confirmation of ordering my steps. During this time, I acknowledge God's track record in my life. I refuse to worry about situations or try to figure them out. Especially when God has ordered my steps. Other times in my room, I devote time to read the word of God and worship Him. I lock my bedroom door and mute my phone. If I forget to tell my family what I am doing, they know when they approach the locked door. While all of what I just shared is effective, I want to model after Jesus and consistently commit the first fruit of my day to Him, and early. Pray for me.

Sister, we cannot do anything absent of God's grace. I used to question if I was "qualified enough" to share the word of God or if I was "good enough" to pray for people. I remember what a preacher said over twenty years ago that began to set me free from the bondage of believing I was unqualified. He said, "God does not call the qualified; He qualifies the called." Earlier, I shared that I had a fear of public speaking and I told God that I trusted Him to deliver me from the bondage of fear. So, I searched scriptures that related to fear and intimidation, meditated on them and applied them to my life. Especially on the occasions when I had to speak in public and pray for others in private. Then, I aligned my faith and belief in the word of God, with subsequent action and His grace prevailed. Faith not supported by action is ineffective. Therefore, when God presented opportunities for me to speak and pray for others, I accepted without hesitation.

In 2014, I was given the opportunity to participate in a prayer call. My assignment was to lead the prayer of thanksgiving bi-monthly and I did so for one year. During this time I was also serving as one of the intercessory prayer leaders at my church. In 2017, I was asked to serve as advisor of a campus ministry called Campus Crusade for Christ (Cru). Not to mention, during that time in my life, God connected me with many people that He would have me to pray for and encourage. I call those moments, divine connections.

In the summer of 2018, I had the honor to share my personal story of transformation with a local church ministry. My prayer sister, Clementine, and her husband lead this ministry and she invited me to share my testimony. So, I did and without skipping a beat I might add. God stretched me in ways I could not imagine or otherwise feel comfortable. The whole process liberated me and challenged me to yield in other areas of my life where I had not allowed myself to be stretched. God showed me that He will use me as a conduit to help someone else be set free from the very thing that had me bound most of my life. He also showed me that my deliverance is in my doing. That, my sister, strengthened me in my walk with Jesus and equipped me in moving closer in my purpose and calling.

The virtuous woman is constantly strengthened especially in her most vulnerable moments. I feared writing this book, but I did it anyway. I was writing another book related to the work I do professionally, but God redirected me to write this one first. I wasn't exactly sure what the process would entail and even what I would say. I thought like some of you may be thinking, I had not lived up to the "virtuous woman" standard of walking in wisdom and excellence. I did not feel the most qualified to write about this woman. I believe God wanted it that way so that I would write this book with zeal and a humbleness to seek Him for wisdom and guidance. I remembered, God qualifies, strengthens and equips those He calls. Scripture says we make plans but the Lord orders our steps.[16] God confirms His word. He will use whatever He chooses to do so and your spirit will bear witness. Trust me, it will.

Since I began writing, God has given me countless confirmations that I am on the right path. Some years ago, a student named Arthur stopped by my office one day and he asked me with such confidence, "Dr. Yorkshire, where is your book?" I was sitting at my desk, looking at my computer as he walked in. Then, I looked at him and replied, "Huh?" He repeated the question without hesitation. "Where is your book?" At that point, I believed God used Arthur to confirm the assignment He gave me. I shared with Arthur that I was in fact, in the process of writing. He said he really thought I had already written and published a book. He further expressed excitement for me and offered to cover me in prayer throughout the process. Another confirmation occurred one day in church several years ago. My Pastor said to me, "You look like an author." I just responded with a smile because he had no idea that I was writing a book.

A couple of years ago, a fellow Deacon at my church asked me to participate in her wedding. As a gift of appreciation, she and her husband gave me a Bible study journal and a beautiful purple mug. On both sides it says, *"You are an Amazing Woman."* The removable lid says, *"Many Women Have Done Excellently, but You Surpass Them All"—Proverbs 31:29!* God does not make mistakes and there is no coincidence in Him. The mug was yet another confirmation that I was to write this book. The couple did not know that I was writing about the virtuous woman and the mug they selected for me could have had many other scriptures engraved on it.

I have colleagues who aspire to be authors. We provide support and encouragement to one another and we hold each other accountable for our writing goals. The Lord has surrounded me and connected me with women who have authored books and shared their stories with the world. How encouraging! Some of them offered to share some insight and guidance to apply along my own journey. Their sharing only ignited my faith as God continued to confirm His will and chart my course.

When I started this writing journey, I did not have an editor or graphic designer. One of my author friends, Jennifer, who unselfishly shared her writing and publishing experience with me, referred some of the experts she previously hired. I reached out to her editor and after speaking with him about the project, I was delighted to move forward. I contacted her publishing design person and while she no longer provides the service, she recommended a local company. I contacted them, answered their questions and voila! I needed a cover design and a former student, Jennyfer, kept coming to mind. I finally contacted her, described my project and I asked her to pray about it. I wanted her to seek God about the cover design and I told her not to rush. A couple of weeks later, she emailed me and part of our dialogue is below.

> Jennyfer: I see an old table, with a beautiful crown without stones . . . this one is optional but having grapes on the table as well . . . the color I think of is purple . . . what are your thoughts?

> Me: What you described sounds very interesting and meaningful. Tell me more about the old table and crown without stones.

> Jennyfer: An antique table symbolizes age, beauty, rarity, condition, social utility, personal emotional connection, or unity/ gathering and connections. A crown without stones symbolizes, to me, honor. We are princesses/queens of the Lord. I will say no stones because we will receive our stones in heaven as rewards for our work. Also, Isaiah 62:3 (NIV) "says, you will be a crown of splendor in the Lord's hands, a royal diadem in the hand of your God." What do you think?

> Me: OMG! This is so GOOD. I was thinking the same thing about the crown. I didn't want to share my thoughts because I wanted to see if we were thinking along the same lines. I had no idea about the table, but I was intrigued to know more about it. YES. . . . l want all of it including the grapes. Grapes in the word of God represents charity (love) and abundance. I'm almost in tears over here because it's all God and I remain in awe of Him.

After additional study we decided to keep the stones (jewels) in the crown. They signify royalty and the crown symbolizes power and authority. I cannot say enough that I remain in awe of God and His faithfulness. Additional confirmations have even shown up "disguised" as some of the challenges I faced while writing this book. Parental challenges, marital challenges, you name it. Through parenting, God has shown me how to forgive and walk in gentleness. I asked Him to help me with my approach and delivery when communicating with my girls so I would not "do too much" as I have been told. He reminded me that sometimes all I need to do is just be attentive and yet silent. God shows us (especially when we ask) when we fall short in parenting our children because such responsibility should not be taken lightly.

The enemy seeks to bring contention and frustration within relationships and certainly with our children. Thank God for discernment and the ability to see in the spirit and to respond accordingly as pleasing to the Lord. Do not provoke them; extend grace and show mercy. As we endeavor to teach them we must also be teachable. No matter how hard things seem to get, God promises that His grace is sufficient. There have been times when I provoked my children and it never ended well or as intended. I have learned to intercede and watch God move in those situations. For instance, there have been times when I did not feel good in my spirit about them going certain places. I used to get upset about it and allow my emotions and authority as their mother to get in the way of having a calm and peaceful conversation. That approach and response usually resulted in an argument, misunderstanding and resentment. The Lord put the scripture in front of me and after meditating on it and yielding to the Holy Spirit, I found that when similar instances presented themselves, instead of my old response, I released it through prayer and trust in God.[17] I mean who would know better how to handle and communicate with my children than Him? The one who created them and selected me to raise them. So, when I responded the new way, it was (and still is) amazing to watch God. Their plans would somehow get canceled or they would ultimately change their minds. In one way or another, something would happen and cause the excitement or strong-willed attitude of my daughters to be reversed.

As a parent, the Lord has shown me that the battle really isn't mine; it is His and has been His all along. If I just get out of His way, because while I am the parent with influence and authority, I am limited but He is limitless. He often reminds me of the power of faith, intercession and bringing my concerns to Him because He cares for me and my children. His faithfulness never runs out. I have seen the fruit notwithstanding bumps along the way. The parenting journey gave me a new respect for the power of prayer and a new level of understanding how to communicate with my girls and nurture my relationship with them. My girls don't always agree with the ways I correct and discipline them but, I believe they will understand that it is always out of love.

Through marital challenges, God has taught me patience, how to communicate more effectively and to extend grace. One day while I was reflecting on the challenges, it hit me like a ton of bricks! God showed me so clearly and prompted me to ask myself, "How could I become *virtuous* if I never faced tough situations (where I needed to apply His Word) and had the lessons learned from each of them? How could I become *virtuous* if I never submitted my will to God and asked Him to order my steps?" The Lord further revealed that I will experience vulnerable moments that require me to trust Him and walk by faith. Wow!

In addition to cultivating her spiritual growth and development because it keeps her in lock step with Him, the virtuous woman knows the importance of having a healthy lifestyle. She is strengthened through proper care of her body; she exercises and rests her mind on things that are good and peaceful. Sometimes I opt to exercise in my house using a weighted hoola hoop, perform jumping jacks or complete sets of crunches. I most enjoy walking my dogs every day. It is very tranquil and allows me to connect with God as I look at nature all around me. During this time of being physically active, I watch the squirrels climb trees and listen to birds chirp while flying overhead. I talk to God and praise Him. I tell Him who He is to me (Waymaker, Promise Keeper, Healer, Creator, and closest friend). I thank Him for healing my mind and my body.

Sister, identify ways to spend time with the Lord. But, you must minimize distractions. I am known to mute my cell phone for hours at a time so that I can "unplug." Sometimes, that focus is as simple as reading a book, exercising or writing this book (smile). Let's face it, there are only so many hours in a day to be productive. I limit unproductive distractions such as watching television. While it may sound easy, it has not been easy for me, but I have noticed the more I do these things, the easier it becomes. I started this book sharing with you how I asked God to renew my mind, and with that, transformation was inevitable. Especially, when I surrendered my will and I yielded to the ways in which God was moving.

The virtuous woman understands that God is going to challenge and stretch her as she grows in her faith. Complacency is a trap set by the enemy. I know about it all too well. God wants us to have an abundant life and the enemy wants to steal it from us or prevent us from experiencing it. He knows how much more dangerous she will be after surrendering to the Lord. By dangerous I mean that much stronger in her walk with Him and thus more effective in her prayer life and in her witness to others. Simply put, when she experiences spiritual growth, transformation has to take place and she can respond to him and his traps boldly and effectively. So, stretching is good. Think about when we exercise our natural bodies. My daughter, Briana, is such a committed exercise accountability partner. She is always that one who suggests that we take time to work-out and she reminds me of our fitness goals. In particular, she reminds me of my personal fitness goals. In response to her nudge, I reluctantly get up and join her.

Stretching my body and putting my limbs under pressure does not feel good. For some of us, working out is not something we want to do most of the time. However, when I take the time to allow my physical muscles to be stretched, it never fails, I always feel so much better after the work-out. Over time, we become stronger and we can see how the exercise has transformed areas of our bodies. Spiritual development is no different, really. In fact, it is more essential for our lives than the physical exercise.[18]

For consideration and action:

What physical activity are you doing? Do you walk, jog, swim or engage in other forms of exercise? Do you settle your mind and direct your thoughts in ways that bring you peace and joy? What could be reflective moments for you? Write them in the spaces below.

I previously stated that God qualifies, strengthens and equips those He calls. How do you know He's calling you? You probably won't feel adequate, experienced or qualified. Recall your prayers. Did they include your YES to Him? Did you ask Him to show you what He wants for your life? If so, you may have followed that question by further asking Him to reveal to you your purpose. Did you ask Him to order your steps? Scripture says we make plans but the Lord orders our steps.[19] Remember what I said earlier, God confirms His word. He will use whatever He chooses to do so and your spirit will bear witness.

Chapter 8

Proverbs 31:18–19

**She perceives that her merchandise is good,
and her lamp does not go out by night.
She stretches out her hands to the distaff,
and her hand holds the spindle.**

The virtuous woman is proud of God's faithfulness in her life. She is confident and unwavering in the work He assigns to her because she prays for wisdom and seeks God for direction. The virtuous woman is resourceful and makes her household and family a priority. Whether she is married or not, with or without children, she understands her position in building her home and covering it in prayer. No matter what storm or trial she faces, her light (the Holy Spirit in her) does not go out and it cannot be hidden. That is because she feeds on the word of God daily and she meditates on His promises. So, when the enemy shows up she is ready for spiritual battle.

The virtuous woman shows hospitality to family members, friends and others as the Lord leads.[20] She might host a gathering and offer to provide refreshments. She opens her home to the family on Thanksgiving, Christmas or Mother's Day. If she has children, she will invite other moms to bring their children over for a play date. If she is married, she and her husband will open their home to other couples for food and fellowship. Ted and I, along with several other married couples at my church completed an assessment on the five love languages. Through that assessment and our sharing, as a group we were able to take-away several things: what is important to our spouses and why, effective communication is essential to being on one accord and it is good to know when the love languages change over time. There are times when we have conversations as a group that have moments of contention around politics, finances and intimacy, just to name a few. But those moments often result in refreshing dialogue and tear-jerking laughter. After it is all said and done, our marriages are strengthened emotionally and spiritually, which is the will of God. Whatever the situation or circumstance, the virtuous woman opens her home to others with love and peace.

Whether amongst friends, family, colleagues, or strangers, the virtuous woman's grace and composure always brings a lighthearted disposition to every room she enters. She provides a safe place and seeks to serve others. She places people before things and offers space for others to exercise their gifts and creativity. She shares what she has and makes time to fellowship with others.

The virtuous woman uses her knowledge of God, His word and her relationship with Him and applies it to her life. As a result, she succeeds. Her success is not defined by the world's standards, expectations and requirements. She reveres the Lord and she is focused on pleasing Him. The virtuous woman asks God to order her steps and reveal her purpose knowing that every assignment He gives her will be in alignment with it.

Some years ago, I was scheduled to attend a professional development event in Philadelphia on a Monday so Ted drove me there a day in advance. While in route, I received a text from a friend and fellow alum, Camille, who asked me if I was interested in being a secretary for a non-profit organization. At the time, I was the secretary for my undergrad's alumni chapter and the scholarship chairperson at my daughters' school. Besides, if that wasn't enough, I was on an advisory council for a female student's mentoring program. I thought, I have enough to do and I am tired. Previously, I asked God to show me the difference between a God-given assignment (connected to my purpose) and a "good idea" that will not bear any eternal fruit. Shortly after texting her some questions about the organization and their expectations, Camille gave me a call. I shared my initial thoughts with her about knowing the difference between God ideas and good ideas and then she replied, "When we identified people to sit on the board a month ago, God dropped you in my spirit." She further stated, "He said, ask Kathy." She said, "I was like Kathy? No, I'm not going to ask her." She explained that someone did accept the secretary position but soon after, rescinded. Then, she heard God again say, "Ask Kathy." She said she no longer wanted to be disobedient as she was clear that God was speaking. Well, during our call, God reminded me of a couple of things:

1. In my prayer time earlier that week and even that morning, I thanked God (in faith) for putting me on someone's mind and I declared His will to be active in my life.

2. I previously desired to join the board of a non-profit organization. However, one day "out of the blue," a colleague invited me to serve on the advisory council for a female student's mentoring program where we work. That wasn't quite what I had in mind (as I desired it) but I recognized God was ordering my steps. So, I accepted the invitation to serve (and I did so for three years) because I believed God was leading me, just not in the way that I initially envisioned. This time, I knew it was my appointed time to serve on the board of a non-profit organization. God was bringing my desire to pass, His way and in His time. Not long after my call with Camille, I started my role as the secretary of Unstoppable You Ministries (UYM). It is an organization that provides resources and support to individuals who experience domestic violence, human trafficking and homelessness. God has used UYM to serve people across the Mid-Atlantic region and I am honored that He chose me to be connected to the vision.

Sister, I consider the aforementioned experience as God's way of taking me through a spiritual assessment. Identifying the difference between what I noted earlier: a God idea (God-given assignment) or a good idea. Our divine assignments may not look the way we envisioned which is really no surprise. After all, His ways are not our ways and His thoughts are higher than ours.[21] How I discern a divine assignment versus a good idea is to ask myself:

1. Does it line up with what God has been speaking to me?

2. Do I have peace about it?

3. Does my spirit bear witness?

4. Does it challenge my disposition of comfort and convenience?

There's more to my list but I'm sure you get the point by now. Also, I constantly examine my "to do" list. It ensures that I am stewarding what God has entrusted me with. Now, don't get me wrong, this does not mean I am less busy but it is imperative that I manage my time in a way that does not let the "Martha spirit" take control of my life.

The virtuous woman is prepared for whatever lies ahead because she abides in the word of God and she is constantly seeking Him for guidance. She endeavors to live out His word in every situation and circumstance. The way God moves in her life is always amazing in her sight and I am convinced, there is nothing better that she could ever experience!

For consideration and action:

What assignments has God given you?	Are you stewarding them well?	How did you determine the difference between just a good idea and a God-given assignment?
1.		
2.		
3.		

Chapter 9

Proverbs 31:20

**She extends her hand to the poor, yes,
she reaches out her hands to the needy.**

The virtuous woman welcomes the work and doesn't mind using her hands. She uses her gifts consistently and creatively as the Lord directs. She's altruistic and benevolent—a philanthropist in her own right. She cannot do everything for everyone but she knows that she can make a difference and do something for someone. Years ago, I set a goal to establish a scholarship and I started one at a community college. I saved up and started with six hundred dollars and in 2017, the Dr. Kathy L. Yorkshire Scholarship was established and to date, four students have been awarded.

Certainly, there are many different ways to show compassion and bless the lives of others. It could be reading books to pre-school kids, donating new and gently used clothes to a local shelter or to someone you know personally that is in need. Also, tutoring someone or volunteering with a literacy program in your community. You could also volunteer your time to serve at an animal shelter by walking the dogs, cleaning rabbit cages and assisting with pet adoptions. The list is endless.

As a parent volunteer at Jasmyn's and Briana's high school, I regularly shared college readiness and scholarship resources with students and their parents. I co-led monthly college preparatory sessions with one of the school counselors. We taught on various topics that helped the students to transition from high school to college.

You might give your time and resources by working in ministry. Perhaps you are responsible for cleaning your church or ensuring the elements are stocked and prepared for Communion. You might teach Sunday school or Bible study. You might even lead a small group in prayer or weekly study of God's word. It is possible that the Lord has you serving those who are not in the church. He may have led you to prepare food and pass it out to the homeless community or visit and pray for residents at a nursing home. Everyone can do something and whatever that is, God can and will use it as a seed that will ultimately lead to a harvest! Whatever your skills and abilities, the Lord will show you how to best use them and in a way that brings Him glory.

For consideration and action:

How are you extending what you have to others? What has God put on your heart? If nothing comes to mind, now is a great time to ask God to show you. Ask Him to connect you with people and opportunities. Your areas of expertise plus your skills and abilities equal ways you can bless others. Write what comes to mind in the spaces below.

Skills + *Abilities* = Ways I can be a blessing to others.

1. _____ + _____ = _____

2. _____ + _____ = _____

3. _____ + _____ = _____

Ask others to add to the list. There are times when people see things in us that we do not see in ourselves. I expect this exercise to be especially enlightening for you. It certainly was for me. Leave blank for now if you are unsure and need to ask God to show you. When He does, don't forget to record it here.

Chapter 10

Proverbs 31:21

**She is not afraid of snow for her household,
for all her household is clothed with scarlet.**

The virtuous woman believes in the power of prayer and she covers her family and her home. Has your mom or someone you know ever said, "Always be prepared for the rainy day that will come?" The virtuous woman endeavors to be organized and prepared for when the storms of life blow. She is resourceful and she desires to steward well everything God has given her. The virtuous woman is the keeper of her home and she is not afraid of trials and tribulations because God warns and instructs her to effectively navigate them and respond accordingly. God proves that He is limitless amidst her limitations. Therefore, she prepares vigilantly and resolves to respond with the right perspective. Instead of complaining about her glass being **half empty**, she is thankful that it is **half full**. On a "rainy day," this is how she chooses to look at her situations and circumstances. She rejoices because of Jesus.

When she faces health challenges she finds promises God has made about wellness and healing. She stands on them and declares them over her life. When she experiences financial loss, she asks God for wisdom and to show her where improvements are needed. Whether it is a new mindset about finances or fundamental steps she needs to take in order to tackle debt. Everything He reveals is to build her character, stretch her faith and to strengthen her testimony for others.

For consideration and action:

How will you become vigilant in your home? How will you prepare for the "rainy day" that will come?

Chapter 11

Proverbs 31:22

**She makes tapestry for herself;
her clothing is fine linen and purple.**

The virtuous woman is intentional about what she makes and also what she wears, physically and spiritually. The words *creates* and *builds* are synonymous to the word *makes*. Whether she creates a way to bless others or if she builds a business, she does not mind putting her hands to task. The virtuous woman is not only creative, she is also clothed in righteousness. Righteousness means to be in right standing with the Lord. Fine linen signifies the righteous acts and ethical conduct of believers of Christ.[22] She knows she can do nothing apart from Him and she looks to Him to be her guide.

I recall one particular occasion when I visited my prayer sister, Clementine's prayer group. It was in the summer of 2018 and as I left the building, we stopped at her car and she presented me with a beautiful purple and white linen dress. Wow! She did not know that I had desired to add purple items to my wardrobe. Side note: a year prior, another prayer sister told me to add purple to my wardrobe because it symbolizes royalty. In the same month that summer, I received a message from someone I previously met at a church service and we stayed in touch. Below is her message, in part:

"Beloved Dr. Kathy, in this month of grace (May) may you experience God's supernatural manifestation like Esther."

Esther 2:17–18 (NIV) [17]Now the king was attracted to Esther more than to any of the other women, and she won his favor and approval more than any of the other virgins. So he set a royal crown on her head and made her queen instead of Vashti. [18]And the king gave a great banquet, Esther's banquet, for all his nobles and officials. He proclaimed a holiday throughout the provinces and distributed gifts with royal liberality.

"Welcome to the month of Grace. Whatever was the error of your life today, by grace, receive divine correction in the mighty name of Jesus. Esther enjoyed love, you will enjoy it too. She also was celebrated. In the name of Jesus you shall be celebrated. I decree and declare this month is your month of Royalty in the mighty name of Jesus."

My response to her, in part:

"Hello Pastor Glory! I receive that in Jesus' name! Wow, you did not know that I just finished studying the story of Esther. I also gave a mini sermon about her in March. Look at God. It's no mistake that He is giving you such word to share with me; it is confirmation. Also, guess what? I received a dress as a gift from my prayer sister, Clementine, and it is purple and white linen. I'm writing a book about the Proverbs 31 woman and verse twenty two says she is clothed in fine linen and purple. Look at God's provision in response to a desire. You are spot on; I am humbled and grateful. God is amazing."

In general, the virtuous woman adorns herself with attire that she is proud to wear. While I relate verse twenty two as more of a personal testimony, it does not mean that you must have purple in your wardrobe. But, why not? For me, it simply lined up with how I was experiencing the Lord's goodness at the time.

For consideration and action:

How might you be experiencing God's goodness in your life right now and how are you adorning yourself physically and spiritually? What are you "wearing" and do you think He is pleased? Write down your thoughts below and talk to God about them.

1. _____
   _____
2. _____
   _____
3. _____
   _____
4. _____
   _____
5. _____
   _____
6. _____
   _____

Hint: Look for the simple here. It does not have to be super deep. My story was about a piece of clothing and its biblical significance.

Chapter 12

Proverbs 31:23

**Her husband is known in the gates,
when he sits among the elders of the land.**

The virtuous woman's husband is recognized in the city or land where he resides. To sit in the gate means to be in a position of authority, decision-making and influence. He is acknowledged for his wisdom. In other words, he is popular and well-respected. The respect, love, and honor the virtuous woman demonstrates towards her husband is a testament to others within their community. This is God's will. It is His will that she sees her husband as He sees him: as a leader, protector, faithful, trustworthy, God-fearing man. When she sees her husband in the flesh she sees faults and deficiencies. Frankly, those are the same things she sees in herself when she walks in the flesh and not by the spirit. However, if she takes those things to God, He will give her and her husband sufficient grace daily.

The virtuous woman understands her role in consistently covering her husband in prayer. She prays with him and she declares the word of God over his life. Scripture says the fervent prayers of the righteous are effective[23] and the virtuous woman is the crown of her husband.[24] She affirms him and does not behave in a manner that shames him. Furthermore, it is her inner strength, courage and dignity that makes him feel humbly proud and honored to be her husband. When I think about the wife I was twenty-one years ago and the wife I am today, I can say without a doubt that God had to show me and teach me how to love my husband unconditionally and how to treat him with the highest honor and respect, right under Him. I learned through prayer and application that I could not control Ted nor protect him in the way I thought was best. That is something that only God can do. God showed me that my influence comes as a result of my steadfast prayers and faith knowing that only He can do what needs to be done in my husband. Other ways I honor my husband:

- Listen and do not talk over him.

- Respect his decisions and trust that he has sought the Lord for wisdom and guidance.

- Cultivate an atmosphere of peace so he can enjoy his home as his sanctuary. Allow him time to regroup after a long, demanding day at work.

- Have dinner planned and prepared (most days, at least). If your husband is the "cook" in the house, consider cleaning the kitchen.

- Virtuous woman, we respect and honor our husbands even as they sit in the gate.

For consideration and action:

If you are married, describe some of the ways you honor your husband. Make note below at least one new way you will begin to honor him. Be sure to hold yourself accountable for this action.

Not married? In what ways will you continue to honor God as a single Christian woman? Remember, this season gives you opportunity and freedom to fully devote yourself to God and His call on your life without having the additional responsibilities of marriage. Also, ask God if it is His will that you marry in the future and if so, ask Him to help you develop the attributes of a virtuous *wife*. The journey of becoming a virtuous woman is certainly a step in the right direction (smile).

1. _____
2. _____
3. _____
4. _____
5. _____
6. _____

Chapter 13

Proverbs 31:24

**She makes linen garments and sells them,
and supplies sashes for the merchants.**

The virtuous woman understands how important it is to try. Many years ago, I attempted to learn how to sew. I took a basic sewing class at a local fabric store and it did not go very well. I was so excited and on the first day of class, I brought all of my supplies ready to create a pair of children's pants. Ultimately, the pants turned out a mess and while I was very disappointed, I was thankful for the experience knowing I tried. The virtuous woman asks God to help her tap into her creative side as well as reveal to her the hidden talents He gave her. In so doing, she is able to identify various ways to earn income, and she does not put all of her "eggs in one basket."

For the past six or so years, I have created my own natural handmade skin and hair care products for my family. In making a conscious effort to live a healthier lifestyle, what we put on our skin and in our hair is important to us. At the time, I stopped using relaxers in my hair and was in the process of learning what my natural hair needed. I purchased many different products and essentially became a product junkie (my fellow naturals know what I mean). Nothing worked well. My hair was in need of conditioning and lasting moisture. One of my daughters had eczema and her skin was irritable. My husband's skin was very dry and coarse and he suffered from painful ingrown hairs. I researched the benefits of different ingredients such as coconut and Vitamin E oils, aloe vera juice, and cocoa butter. After experimenting for quite some time, I created skin and hair products that worked for us.

One year, I gifted my handmade products to women on Mother's Day and to some people on their birthdays. Many of them asked if I was selling them. Some offered to buy my products when they ran out of their gifted items. I had a desire to start a business but I wanted something simple and not overly complicated. Moreover, I wanted to do something that met a need. So, I asked God to guide my steps and to reveal my business at the right time if it was His will. It was important for me to be intentional with my decisions using Godly wisdom.

While driving to church one morning, I told Ted that I wanted a simple business that could meet a great need for men and women. We began to discuss possible business names. Ted remarked, "Simply . . . simple" and with excitement, I shouted "Simply Pure and Authentic!" followed by "A Natural Spa Experience" as the tagline. Check out the play on SPA which are acronyms for the name. Yes! I knew that was it! However, I was a doctoral student in addition to being a wife and mother of two. The goal of pursuing this dream of becoming a successful entrepreneur did not end at that point of realization. But, I recalled my prayer for wisdom and guidance and I pressed the "pause" button until I graduated. Upon completing my degree, I officially launched Simply Pure and Authentic, LLC: A Natural Spa Experience.

The virtuous woman is a homemaker with entrepreneurial skills, abilities and endeavors. She is creative and does not mind working with her hands to produce that which others not only need but enjoy. In earlier verses, we learned about her homemaking. Being an effective homemaker first is essential and those characteristics and skills will transcend into business ownership. In chapter three, I explained how I started a resume writing business in an earlier season in my life. In latter seasons, I stepped into other business ventures including real estate and inventing a natural hair and skincare product line. All of it allowed me to tap into my leadership skills and creative side. Not to mention, I earned additional income while doing it.

For consideration and action:

How are you creating multiple streams of income? Haven't started yet? What has God revealed to you and what do you need to start? Do you believe God is leading you to be an entrepreneur using your skills and gifts to bless your household, family and perhaps, the world? Write your responses in the spaces on the next page.

$Coaching/Consulting/Writing$_____

$Designing$_____

$Teaching/Tutoring$ _____

$Consigning/Reselling$ _____

$Other$ _____

Now, ask the Lord for guidance. Notice the following prayer prompt I provided to get you started.

Lord Jesus,

Thank you for ordering my steps each and every day. I know that I have not always followed your lead and I am sorry for my disobedience. I am grateful to know that you are a forgiving and loving God who wants only the best for me. You will also use everything that I have been through to work together for my good. I'm ready to set down my will and be led by your Spirit. I know you have more for me and I believe part of it is_____. You have given me talents and gifts that I can use to bless others. Lord, show me how those things may be used to be a financial blessing to my family and this world. Help me to see the subtle hints in the confirmation and provision you place before me. Lord, cause me to see the "trees" and the "forest." You promised to always be with me. Therefore, I trust you and I am excited about what you are going to do going forward and the ways you will make. Thank you, Jesus, for helping me to get out of my own way! I give you all honor and glory!

Amen, amen and amen.

Chapter 14

Proverbs 31:25

**Strength and honor are her clothing;
she shall rejoice in time to come.**

The virtuous woman is thankful to God in everything no matter the circumstances. I don't know about you but "wearing" strength and dignity has not come easy for me. I did not feel very strong or have true confidence until I understood who I was in Christ. Whenever the enemy devises schemes to set me back in that place of bondage, I declare the word of God in the face of his lies. I praise Jesus for who He is and for everything He has already done for me. Didn't I say earlier that His track record is unmatched? There will be days in which you may not feel so strong or confident but, praise the Lord anyway! Think about how far He has brought you and remember God promises that His grace is sufficient.[25] He also promises to make all things work together for the good of those of us who love Him and are called according to His purpose.[26]

The virtuous woman waits for God to manifest His promises in her life. Many times I did not wait on God. I was impatient and foolish enough to believe God needed my help. What a joke! Really? I have come to know and understand that I am limited but God is limitless. His timing is always better than mine. I can do nothing apart from Him and His track record with me is unmatched. In case you haven't noticed, I keep repeating this for a reason.

When my oldest daughter, Jasmyn, was completing her senior year of high school, I refused to worry about how Ted and I would pay for her first semester of college. In addition to what we saved, my mother's contribution and a couple of small scholarships awarded to Jasmyn, we still did not have all that was needed to cover the remaining amount. The word of God tells us to cast our cares on Him because He cares for us.[27] It also tells us to be still, know that He is God and to wait for Him.[28] I thanked God for His provision and I trusted Him because I know if He didn't make a way, there would be no way.

Less than six months before it was time for Jasmyn to go to college, I was asked if I had interest in teaching a new course in addition to my regular course load and I accepted the offer. One day as I calculated everything including tuition, housing and fees, I realized the amount needed to cover her first semester balance (not including what we saved, received from my mom and the small scholarships) equaled the compensation I would receive for the additional course. It hit me like a ton of bricks. Now, that's provision! I was and continue to be in awe at the faithfulness of God. Sometimes in our stillness, we must not waver in what we believe and trust in the one who created us because His word never fails.

God equips the virtuous woman to take on challenges. She draws her strength from the Holy Spirit. Therefore, she can approach her future with confidence because the Lord has shown His faithfulness to her and I have shared many of my own personal stories with you to prove it. That faithfulness gives her assurance to smile at her future. She knows God has called her to live for such a time as this and to partner with Him in the work He created her to perform. Each day she is allowed to see, she recognizes it is a gift from God and she makes the choice to be glad and rejoice. We say God is a WAYMAKER, MIRACLE WORKER, HEALER AND PROMISE KEEPER. Why do we have such a hard time believing it? We do not humble ourselves enough to change our attitudes about the goodness and grace of God. Our hope is in other people and we don't really believe that His grace is sufficient. I know the times when I didn't. God commanded us to humble ourselves, pray, and walk by faith because our hope is in Him alone. God said anything is possible if we have faith the size of a mustard seed.[29] Have you seen a mustard seed lately?

For consideration and action: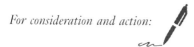

Write down two seemingly impossible situations where only God can intervene. Include at least one scripture that you will meditate on as it relates directly to each situation.

Situation #1:

Scripture:

Trust God

Situation #2:

Scripture:

Chapter 15

Proverbs 31:26

**She opens her mouth with wisdom,
and on her tongue is the law of kindness.**

The virtuous woman is humble and chooses her words carefully; they are gracious, kind and gentle. Kindness sets a positive, secure atmosphere that does not intimidate others. She understands to be kind is a choice. Let's face it, making such a choice can be a challenging action for many of us to demonstrate in our daily lives. However, God resists the proud and gives grace to the humble.[30]

The Bible says pleasant words are sweet like a honeycomb.[31] The virtuous woman has a tactful way to respond and offer insight when requested and unsolicited. She is slow to speak, but her words are purposeful and powerful. Wisdom is the fruit of her lips and if married, she comforts her husband when he feels the weight of the world on his shoulders. She lifts him with encouragement and prayer during his lowest moments. The virtuous woman loves her husband unconditionally. This has been a process for me and I am still learning while working to be gentle to my husband. I was not always the kindest wife and I do not always speak pleasantly as I should. God shows me in His word and during my devotional time that harsh and spiteful words do not bear good fruit.[32] That's right, they don't produce positive outcomes, period. Such attitude and actions often turn into a petty argument that results in remorse. Teachable moments happen when God reveals His best for me and my marriage. My relationship with Him must be strong first and that is when I can ensure the strength of my relationship with my husband. My husband and I, together with God, ensure our success because He promised that a threefold cord is not easily broken.[33]

With all the negativity in this world, how does the virtuous woman walk in humility and speak with kind, gentle and wise words? How we say things is powerful because they build up and they can condemn. They can speak life and death to and about others.[34] Therefore, she meditates on the word of God and when she does not, her words are sharp, hurtful and unfruitful. God tells us to meditate on His word day and night.[35] That means to think about the word, study it, believe it, and apply it to our lives daily. The virtuous woman demonstrates Godly character because she has learned to guard her heart. She cannot guard her heart if she does not meditate on the word of God. Whatever she is going through, she finds scriptures related to her situation and she meditates on them and prays. She is careful about what she listens to and what she watches on television. She does not indulge in all conversations unless she is led by the Holy Spirit to do so. As we work to develop Godly characteristics, we must understand what prevents us from being effective such as unconstructive criticism, complaining and unbelief. Scripture says what we speak reveals what is in our hearts.[36]

What opportunity have you had to speak kindly to someone who wasn't very kind to you? Notice, I said *opportunity*. Did you seize it or did you allow criticism, complaining and unbelief win? Have you had a chance to share your knowledge and wisdom with others so they could be corrected in love, encouraged and strengthened? When was the last time you found yourself being tested and in that moment you understood the need to speak with gracious words? Give yourself room to try and try again. It is not the end of the world to fall short. God already knows we will but He did promise to give us grace to start anew. Past experiences (based on what we saw and heard), and perhaps a lifetime of responding to situations opposite of God's way will take some of us longer to let go. Therefore, we should not expect changes in our behavior to be an "overnight success." The process of being transformed by the renewing of our minds takes time. It takes intentional and consistent effort to let go of our will and to seek and submit to God's will. That is what wisdom, humility, and graciousness looks like.

For consideration and action:

What words have you spoken recently? Fill in the spaces below.

Kind Word	1. _____	2. _____
Wise Word	1. _____	2. _____
Correcting Word	1. _____	2. _____

Chapter 16

Proverbs 31:27

**She watches over the ways of her household,
and does not eat the bread of idleness.**

The virtuous woman considers her home her sanctuary. She is careful to observe how her house operates because she is devoted to doing things that make it a home. She asks herself, "Does my home offer a welcoming and peaceful atmosphere to everyone who enters?" The virtuous woman creates an environment that is nurturing and safe. She sets the tone and encourages others to flourish and prosper. That could be represented by lending a listening ear, sharing a word of wisdom or even a word of correction that is spoken in love.

She is energetic enough to carry out tasks and when that is not the case, she makes time to examine her life and balance her priorities. I previously shared with you just how I do this in order to prevent the "Martha spirit" from taking over my life on any given day. The virtuous woman spends time with God in order to refocus and refuel because she has come to understand that taking a Sabbath is necessary for her spiritual, mental and physical well-being. Don't misunderstand me, Martha loved and honored Jesus. That was evident by the way she focused on serving Him while He was at Martha and Mary's home. However, at that time, it was more important to Him for Martha to sit at His feet with Mary so He could speak to her heart as well.

As the keeper of her home as first mentioned Chapter 5, the virtuous woman may hire someone to help with household responsibilities because whatever she decides, she recognizes the benefits and she prioritizes execution. I know a woman who has a seven member family unit. She expressed how laundry had become a source of contention. After speaking with her husband about it, they agreed to hire a woman at their local laundromat to launder their clothes every few weeks. As a result, there is no more contention and stress around the topic of laundry. Furthermore, she is freed up a bit to focus on other tasks and responsibilities including spending time alone in the presence of God.

Do you ever feel like you don't have enough time in the day? The virtuous woman manages her time wisely by prioritizing her tasks. She has self-discipline and she is discerning when it comes to how she responds to opportunities. She knows when to say no to "good" ideas that were not presented by God. She is diligent to pray for her household, family and their well-being. She is not lazy and unproductive in her natural and spiritual life. As a single woman, she manages her home well and declares His promises with expectation that God will not allow them to return void.[37] Her primary focus is to walk in her calling and ministry. She resists the temptation to believe that she is not going to be the woman of God she was created to be no matter the season.

For consideration and action: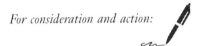

How do I describe my household and its environment? What do I desire it to be and how can I make improvements?

Areas of my household that need improvements	Solutions/ Remedies	Start Date	Next Step(s)

Chapter 17

Proverbs 31:28–29

**Her children rise up and call her blessed;
her husband also, and he praises her.
Many daughters have done well,
but you excel them all.**

The virtuous woman loves her children enough to discipline them when they need to be corrected. She also encourages them and instills hope in God, His grace and His unlimited power in their lives. The virtuous woman's husband understands that she is the woman God called him to love unto death. The virtuous woman does not worship her husband's every move and she is not a "yes" woman that agrees with all of his decisions. She respects his position of leadership and she offers him encouragement. God showed me where I fell short. He showed me where I wanted to be in control and when I walked in pride. All of us fall short and we should seek Him for wisdom. Now, I go before the Lord (well, most times) to lay my thoughts and feelings before Him. He already knows what is in my heart, I might as well share it with the one who can actually help me with no strings attached; just His love, mercy and grace.

Perhaps you are not married or don't have children. Consider those around you. The individuals you work with, worship and do business with should call you blessed based on the way you have made a difference in their lives. Sister, acknowledge God's headship over your life as He enables you to do the work He's created and called you to do. God desires that you experience His sovereignty in your life while being assured that even in your season of not being married or raising children, you are never alone. God intends for each one of us to live out our purpose knowing that we are responding to His call. Remember the gifts of the spirit (also known as spiritual gifts) first mentioned in Chapter two? I am not a certified parental or marital expert but these things have proven to be effective in my relationship with my girls and in my marriage. While I have learned a lot, I continue to learn as the Spirit leads.

For consideration and action:

How do you want to be known and remembered based on the way you have blessed the people in your life? Fill in the spaces below and refer to them regularly to examine whether or not your actions line up with them.

Chapter 18

Proverbs 31:30

**Charm is deceitful and beauty is passing,
but a woman who fears the Lord, she shall be praised.**

The virtuous woman is not interested in pretending to be something she is not. As she matures in Christ, those days of being phony and surface-level are put behind her. She is a woman on a mission to do the will of Jesus and that includes being a witness of His love and faithfulness. The virtuous woman understands the importance of making critical decisions and she seeks the Lord for wisdom and guidance. She knows it is only to her detriment and perhaps even to others, to lean to her own understanding. Therefore, she fears God with a reverential kind of fear. She is careful to discern what God is saying and doing in her life. The point is that having Godly character is the focus of the virtuous woman. When God gives her an assignment, particularly a challenging assignment, her ultimate response is that of thanksgiving and praise because she knows His grace is sufficient and it is an opportunity for Him to get the glory.

God shows us His sovereignty in our situations and circumstances. Some consider a challenge as a way that He tests our faith and others consider a challenge as an opportunity to strengthen our faith. In any case, God wants us to recognize when His hand is moving versus our own. He also desires that through the process of building and strengthening our faith, He wants us to take an inward look and perspective about our attitudes because they can dictate our responses. It is by faith and through our obedience to God's direction that we can operate in peace and fullness of joy. It is not always going to be an easy thing to do and it's not meant to be. It is through the hardship and the struggle that the virtuous woman realizes her God given strength and fortitude in believing that He is shaping her into the woman He created her to be. Especially in the earth and in her service to others. Flaws and all! While writing this book, I have faced situations and circumstances where I had to see the test, "stand" in the middle of it and make a spiritual withdrawal of all that God has deposited in me. His track record is unmatched. His faithfulness is certain and there's never been a fight that He did not win. I have seen Him prevail in my life time and time again. For every "win" I have seen Him perform, my faith has been strengthened even more. The battles are never mine, they are always His.

The virtuous woman is not perfect, nor does she expect to be. However, she uses her faults and shortcomings as teachable moments that God gives her so she can grow. Therefore, there is no experience she has that is ever wasted. She is confident that God uses all of her situations and circumstances as opportunities to stretch her beyond her natural abilities. She can only accomplish that with the Holy Spirit. In so doing, her faith, confidence, and reliance on God increases exponentially. That is because she knows there is no failure in Him. The virtuous woman is a model of wisdom and excellence in the eyes of God. She is honorable, gracious and resilient and there is nothing or no one that can take those things away from her.

For consideration and action:

What was the last situation where you felt tested by God? I won't ask if you passed the test. Rather, I wonder how your faith was strengthened by it. In the box below, list at least one thing you will do first when another "testing" situation shows up.

Chapter 19

Proverbs 31:31

**Give her of the fruit of her hands,
and let her own works praise her in the gates.**

The virtuous woman works willingly with her hands and she does not grumble while completing her tasks. Her life-long actions speak for themselves. The results of her diligence (as a result of the fruit of her hands) and perseverance is evident in her life. She is honored and recognized by those who know her. This is because she has proven to be a blessing to them. She has prayed for them, said a kind word, gave a gentle hug or met an extrinsic need. The virtuous woman is constantly evolving into the woman God created her to be. She endeavors to do good and she pursues His wisdom and peace. It is her desire and daily pursuit to live out God's word in her life, not just merely read about what He can do and quote it. Living it out is demonstrated by the word being in her heart and her willingness to walk in humility and thus, God gets the glory! You may ask, "What is giving God glory?" It is when credit is given but it can only be given to Him because we are just not that powerful or smart. Oh, what a special feeling of joy and peace we feel when we know we were used by God and when His sovereignty is revealed, as a result.

God has shown me that if I abide in Him, He will abide in me.[38] That goes for you, too. I thank Him so much as He has given me clear insight about my challenges (like the fear described earlier) and how to respond to them. When I have yielded to the challenges, I have witnessed God's plans for me. I desired to draw closer to Him and take a step. I asked God to renew my mind and during that renewal process, He made it so clear that I needed to seek Him first! So I had to reprioritize and begin to make changes as I abided in Him and Him in me. God has changed the trajectory of my life and it has been an amazing season although, not without a fight from the enemy! But, the Lord prevailed every time and that has enabled me to walk in more boldness and confidence. My prayer circle has widened with an increase in powerful prayer partners. As believers, we experience transformation over the course of our lives. It's a change; a new way of thinking and behaving made possible through the power of the Holy Spirit. God gives us commands throughout scripture for us to renew our minds and to be transformed which includes getting rid of our old and unfruitful ways of thinking. He knew how powerful it would be for us, not to mention the glory He would get.

The virtuous woman, a woman of strength and noble character. She embodies faith and wisdom within her home, community and relationships. The Lord empowers her to be a source of light in darkness and steadfast in challenging times. The virtuous woman is not perfect and she was never created to be by any means. However, she is bold and confident because she knows the Lord is with her at all times. If you haven't discovered it by now, **they are secrets of becoming a virtuous woman**. But, they are not the kind of secrets to keep to yourself. Go and tell others! Sister, God created you and He's calling you for such a time as this to become a virtuous woman. Will you accept the call? If yes, now is the time to take the first step. If you have never accepted Jesus Christ as your personal Lord and Savior (see Romans 10:9–10), pray the following prayer of salvation with me:

> *Lord Jesus, I have lived my life MY way for too long and I am sorry. I am a sinner in need of salvation. I believe in my heart that you died for my sins and that God raised you from the dead so that I might have everlasting life. Therefore, I invite you to come into my heart and save me. Thank you for loving me so much that you would offer me the gift of salvation, the promise of eternal life. I happily and humbly accept. I am excited about my new life; my new life with you as my Lord and Savior, Jesus Christ, that starts now. Amen!*

Romans 10:9–10 (AMP):

[9]because if you acknowledge *and* confess with your mouth that Jesus is Lord [recognizing His power, authority, and majesty as God], and believe in your heart that God raised Him from the dead, you will be saved. [10]For with the heart a person believes [in Christ as Savior] resulting in his justification [that is, being made righteous—being freed of the guilt of sin and made acceptable to God]; and with the mouth he acknowledges *and* confesses [his faith openly], resulting in *and* confirming [his] salvation.

I am so excited for you, your new life and your new journey! As you follow Jesus and live for Him, get ready for some amazing twists and turns. If you haven't done so already, get in a Godly community where you can learn the word of God and be supported through biblical teaching, discipleship and prayer. Ask God to connect you with a church and other believers so that you can continue to grow. Now, join me and your other sisters in Christ in saying the following prayer:

Lord Jesus, thank you for loving us the way you do. Your love toward us is constant and we cannot thank you enough. You are a forgiving God; one who gives us additional chances to walk up right before you. You keep us daily. Even in our mess when we are not so loving or lovable. No one can love us the way you do. No one. We are sorry for not consistently putting you first and above all else. Thank you for giving us another chance. While this book is entitled Secrets of Becoming a Virtuous Woman, *it really is no secret once we know and understand who we are as the women of God you created us to be. Lord, we apologize for not always acknowledging our call. Forgive us for not looking to you as our source for everything. Lord, we ask you at this very moment to begin to transform us by the renewing of our minds. We want all that you have for us and for those we are connected to. Therefore, we surrender our will and accept your will for our lives. Now that the secret's out, today, we say* **yes**. *It is in your mighty and matchless name Jesus, that we seal this prayer. Amen!*

Connect with the Author:

Email: kathy@virtuouswomentoday.com

Website: www.virtuouswomentoday.com

IG: @virtuous.women.today

Notes

Endnotes

1. Romans 12:2
2. Matthew 6:33
3. Revelation 3:8
4. James 2:17
5. Matthew 6:33
6. Proverbs 16:3
7. Proverbs 18:22
8. Matthew 18:20
9. Isaiah 54:5
10. 1 Corinthians 12:4–11
11. 1 Corinthians 12:7
12. James 1:5
13. Proverbs 3:6
14. Proverbs 16:9
15. Romans 8:28
16. Proverbs 16:9
17. Ephesians 6:4
18. 1 Timothy 4:8
19. Proverbs 16:9
20. 1 Timothy 5:10
21. Isaiah 55:8–9
22. Revelation 19:7–8
23. James 5:16
24. Proverbs 12:4
25. 2 Corinthians 12:9
26. Romans 8:28
27. 1 Peter 5:7
28. Psalm 46:10
29. Matthew 17:20
30. James 4:6
31. Proverbs 16:24
32. Proverbs 15:1
33. Ecclesiastes 4:12
34. Proverbs 18:21
35. Joshua 1:8
36. Luke 6:45
37. Isaiah 55:11
38. John 15:4

Made in the USA
Middletown, DE
05 March 2023